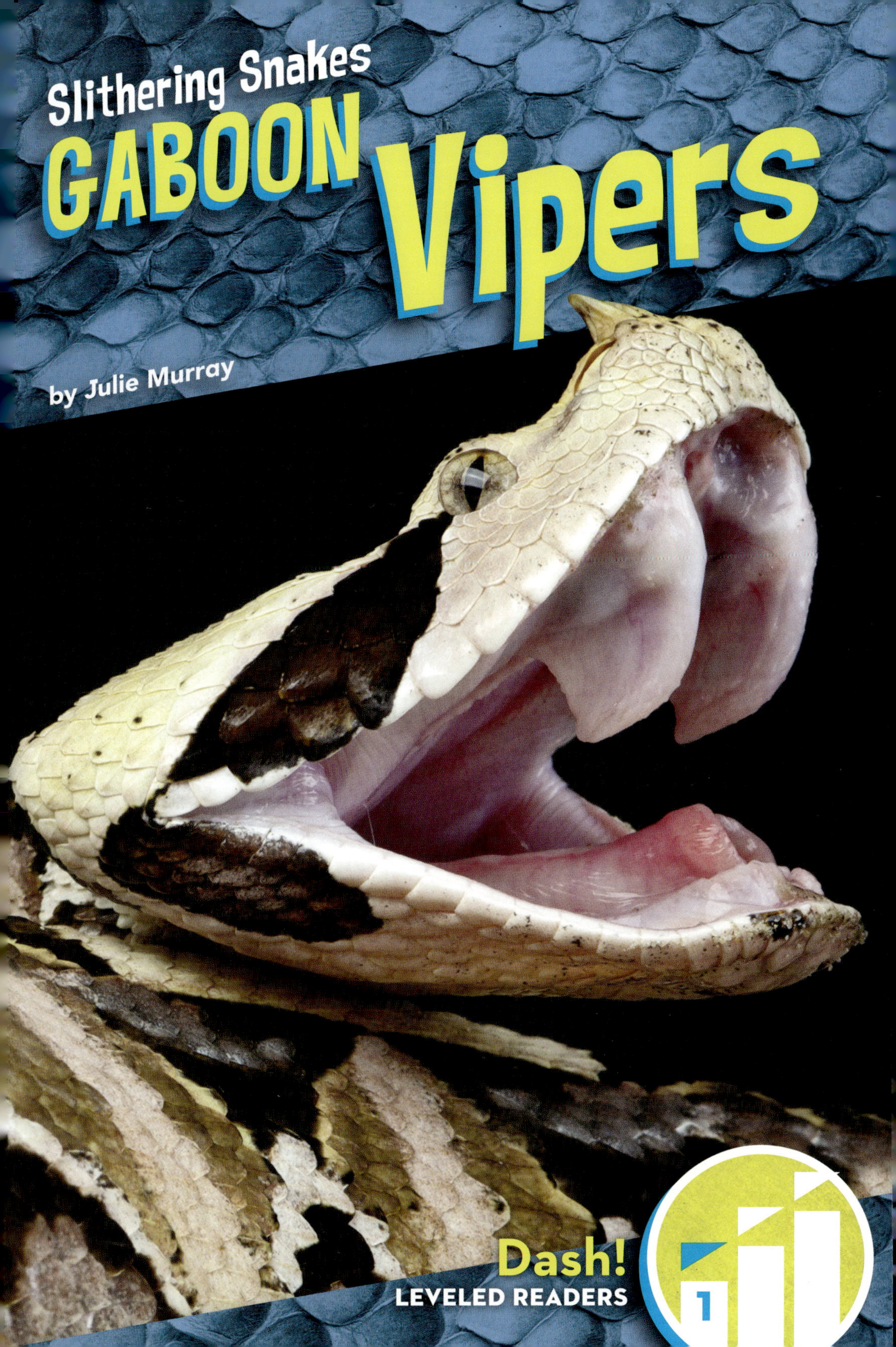
Slithering Snakes
GABOON Vipers
by Julie Murray
Dash!
LEVELED READERS
1

Level 1 – Beginning
Short and simple sentences with familiar words or patterns for children who are beginning to understand how letters and sounds go together.

Level 2 – Emerging
Longer words and sentences with more complex language patterns for readers who are practicing common words and letter sounds.

Level 3 – Transitional
More developed language and vocabulary for readers who are becoming more independent.

abdopublishing.com

Published by Abdo Zoom, a division of ABDO, P.O. Box 398166, Minneapolis, Minnesota 55439.

Printed in the United States of America, North Mankato, Minnesota.
092017
012018

Photo Credits: Alamy, iStock, National Geographic Creative, Shutterstock
Production Contributors: Kenny Abdo, Jennie Forsberg, Grace Hansen, John Hansen
Design Contributors: Dorothy Toth, Neil Klinepier

Publisher's Cataloging in Publication Data

Names: Murray, Julie, author.
Title: Gaboon Vipers / by Julie Murray.
Description: Minneapolis, Minnesota: Abdo Zoom, 2018. | Series: Slithering snakes | Includes online resource and index.
Identifiers: LCCN 2017939244 | ISBN 9781532120732 (lib.bdg.) | ISBN 9781532121852 (ebook) | ISBN 9781532122415 (Read-to-Me ebook)
Subjects: LCSH: Gaboon Vipers--Juvenile literature. | Snakes--Juvenile literature. | Reptiles--Juvenile literature.
Classification: DDC 597.96--dc23
LC record available at https://lccn.loc.gov/2017939244

Table of Contents

Gaboon Vipers

Gaboon vipers live in Africa. They are very dangerous!

Africa

They can be found in **rain forests**. They live on the ground.

They are big snakes! They can be 6 feet (1.8 m) long and weigh 25 pounds (11 kg)!

Their heads are shaped like a triangle. They have two horns.

Their scales are pale and brown in color.

Their scales make a cool **pattern**!

Their **fangs** can be 2 inches (5 cm) long! The fangs release **venom**.

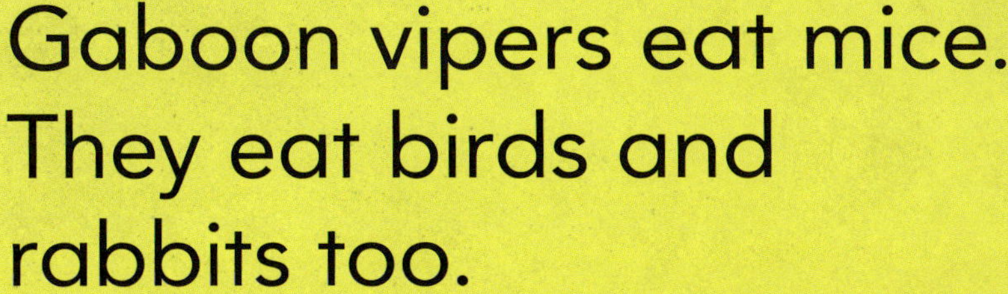

Gaboon vipers eat mice. They eat birds and rabbits too.

They can live for 18 years in the wild.

More Facts

- Gaboon vipers are the largest vipers in the world.
- They can lie still for months waiting for a meal.
- They have the longest **fangs** of any snake.

Glossary

fang – a long, pointed tooth that is used to bite prey and inject venom.

pattern – an arrangement of repeated markings.

rain forest – a forest mostly found in tropical areas that receive a large amount of rain all year long.

venom – the poison that certain snakes produce.

Index

Online Resources

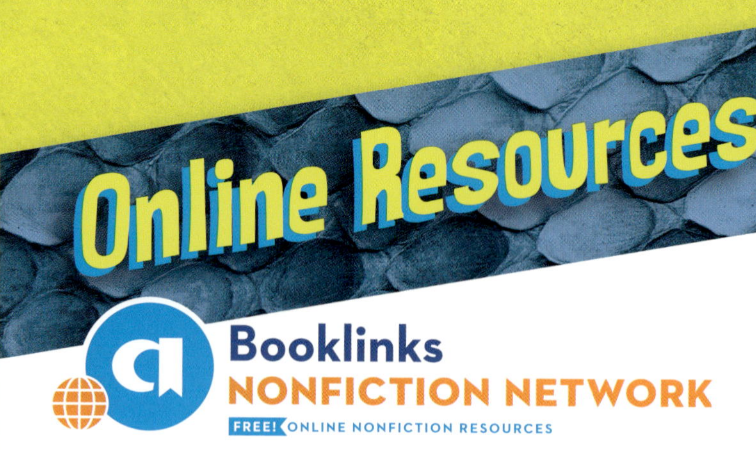

To learn more about Gaboon vipers, please visit **abdobooklinks.com**. These links are routinely monitored and updated to provide the most current information available.